Catriona

Many and strange are the tales that are told by the men of Northland as they sit by their great log fires.

None is stranger than the tale of how Noggin saw the face of his bride on the white bone knife which the green bird brought him, and how he sailed beyond the black ice at the edge of the world to bring her home from the Land of the Midnight Sun.

The adventures that befell him on the journey, and how, at last, the evil schemes of Nogbad the Bad were foiled, are told in this, the first tale in the Saga of Noggin the Nog.

The Saga of Noggin the Nog

1. KING OF THE NOGS
2. THE ICE DRAGON
3. THE FLYING MACHINE
4. THE OMRUDS
5. THE ISLAND
6. THE FIRECAKE
7. THE PIE
8. THE FLOWERS
9. THE GAME
10. THE MONSTER

For Hannah

First published by
KAYE & WARD LTD
21 New Street, London EC2M 4NT
1968
Reprinted 1969, 1974

ISBN 0 7182 0290 2

Printed in England by Jarrold & Sons Ltd, Norwich

THE : SAGA : OF : NOGGIN : THE : NOG

KING of the NOGS

BY : OLIVER · POSTGATE & PETER · FIRMIN

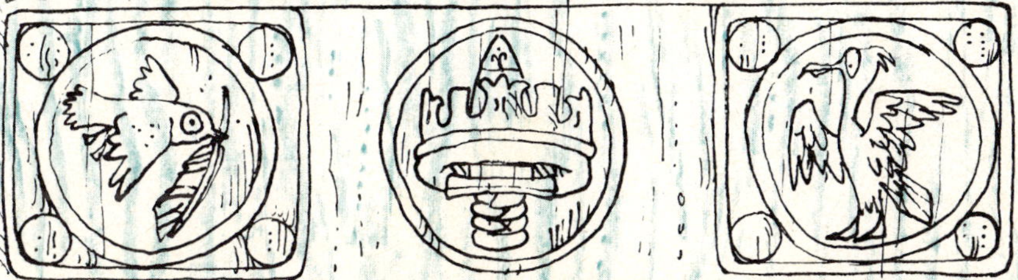

KAYE & WARD Ltd, 21. NEW STREET, LONDON, E.C.2

In the lands of the North, where the black rocks stand guard against the cold sea, in the dark night that is very long, the Men of the Northlands sit by their great log fires and they tell a tale.

They tell of a prince and how he built a long ship and sailed beyond the black ice at the edge of the world to bring home his bride from the land of the Midnight Sun.

Noggin the Nog was the name of the prince. He was the son of Knut, King of the Nogs, the aged ruler of that land of dark forest and snow which men call the land of Nog.

Now, every morning King Knut would rise from his bed, put on his boots and climb to the hill above the royal castle. At the top of this hill was a rock known as Knut's seat. The aged king would sit on the seat and as the sun rose behind the mountains he would begin to worry.

He would look down on the little town clustered around the castle walls and he would worry about his people and whether their roofs leaked and whether they had warm socks this cold weather. He would look down on his castle and he would worry about his son, Prince Noggin, and what would happen to his people if Noggin did not marry soon; for it is the law in the North-land that the king shall be married. The old king knew that if he died Noggin would have to marry within six weeks of his death or he would not become king, and then the crown would go to his wicked uncle, Nogbad the Bad.

The people of the town would look up at their king sitting there worrying and they would say, "Don't worry old king", but of course the king would go on worrying just the same.

Then, one day, the king rose from his seat as if to go down to his castle. The people watching him saw him shake and stagger and fall to the ground. The king was dead. Great was the sadness and loud the wailing. The flags on the houses were pulled to half mast and the great bell rang. All were sad, save one. In his black castle Nogbad the Bad heard the distant sounds of sorrow and smiled a greedy smile.

In the Royal Castle, Noggin's mother, Queen Grunhilda rose from her bed and called for the prince.

"Noggin," she said, "the time has come for you to choose a bride. I shall summon all the maidens of gentle birth to the castle within seven days, and on the seventh day you shall choose your bride."

Soon the sound of trumpets was heard throughout the land as, from the battlements of the castles, from the balconies of the tallest houses the royal heralds proclaimed their message.

What excitement there was among the maidens! What twittering and giggling! With hopeful hearts they put on their walking shoes and skipped away to the Royal Castle.

On the seventh day, the maidens assembled, dozens of them, in lines across the hall. Slowly Noggin the Nog walked along the lines looking with great care and friendliness. There were tall girls, short girls, lean girls from the valleys with hair as black as ravens' wings, fat girls from the castles of the mountain top with golden plaits and eyes as blue as the sky.

Noggin came to the end of the line and he

had not chosen. He had not found one maiden that pleased him enough to make her his queen.

Standing calmly next to the very last maiden of all, Noggin saw a large green bird, a strange bird, the like of which he had never seen before.

"You are not a maiden, you are a bird," he said.

"Your highness is observant," said the bird and he bowed.

"My name is Graculus. I have flown from

the land of the Midnight Sun and from my master, Nan of the Nooks, I bring you greetings and a gift." The bird took from under his wing a knife. He placed it in Noggin's hand.

"Thank you very much," said Noggin. He looked at the knife. It was made from a single faultless walrus tooth. In the middle of the blade was carved the likeness of a girl's face. Noggin looked at the face and he thought it beautiful, more beautiful than any of the maidens he had seen that day, or any other day for that matter.

"Who is this maiden?" he asked.

"It is the likeness of my master's daughter," said the bird. "It is the face of Nooka, Princess of the Nooks."

Noggin, Prince of the Nogs, turned to his people and, holding up the knife, he cried out, "This is the maiden I shall marry."

What alarm and surprise there was in the castle! What grumbling and grumping! With heavy hearts the maidens put on their walking shoes and trudged back to their homes.

Noggin climbed the steps in the castle yard and addressed the Royal Guard and the people of the town.

"Who will come with me?" he asked.

"We will!" cried the warriors with one voice.

"Who will build me a ship?" he asked.

“We will!” called the carpenters.

“And we will paint it!” called the painters.

“And we will make you sails!” called the sailmakers.

And so it was. The Nogs built a long ship of oak from the valleys. The mast was a single perfect pine tree. The high prow was carved and painted and gilded to a ferocious dragon's head. The sail was a square of stout canvas embroidered with the crest of Noggin and the face of Nooka. To protect the sides of the ship were shields of hammered bronze.

"Do not grieve for me, Mother," said Noggin the Nog as he took leave of Queen Grunhilda. "The ship is strong, the men are brave. Graculus

will guide us through the perils of the deep."

So the ship was launched. Noggin and his band of warriors raised the great square sail with the crest of Noggin and the face of Nooka. The wind took the sail and the ship moved away down the fjord towards the sea.

The people watched from the quay and waved goodbye. Everybody was sad to see them go and afraid for their safety on the long and perilous journey. Everybody save one.

In his black castle on the hill, Nogbad the Bad looked down on the little ship and he smiled. He knew that the journey to the land of the Midnight Sun was so long and dangerous that there was little chance of Noggin coming back and, as he thought of the royal treasure, the taxes and jewels and the crown which would soon be his, he chuckled to himself.

"Huh. Huh. Huh!"

A good wind blew the ship away from the land of Nog. Night came. The helmsman lashed the steering oar to hold the helm to the North Star and the band of Nogs sat round their stove in the canvas cabin and made hot buttered toast.

All the next day and night the wind blew them on. Then, one day, the wind dropped. The sun came out and it was really quite warm.

As the sun set that night a storm blew up. The wind howled in the rigging. The thunder roared, the lightning flashed as the great waves tossed the little ship about like a cork.

Graculus lay under a shelf feeling very very sick. The Nogs huddled around their stove and prayed that the ship would not sink.

Morning came. The storm blew past and all was calm. They hoisted the sail and looked at it. No wind came to fill it. It hung limp on the mast and the ship stayed where it was, still in a

calm still sea.

The Captain of the Guard, the fierce Thor Nogson, stood at the helm.

"What do we do now, Noggin?" he asked.

"Row, I suppose," replied the prince.

The oarsmen took up their oars.

"Which way do we row?" asked Thor Nogson.

"Oh dear, I don't know," said Noggin the Nog.

They could not ask Graculus: he was too sea-sick to talk. So the Nogs got out their fishing rods and sat in the sun and

fished. They did not catch anything but it passed the time.

"Land Ho!" came a shout from the look-out.

Not much land indeed, just a small, smooth brownish grey island in the sea.

"Row that way," said Noggin.

They rowed over to the island and Thor Nogson swung out on a rope and landed on it.

"Ooh, it's all soft and squodgy," he said,

"and it's covered with sort of brown grass stuff."

"Explore the island," said Noggin.

"Explore it? I can see all of it from where I am standing! There is nothing here except this brown grass stuff."

"Dig some up," said Noggin.

They threw Thor Nogson a spade. He put it to the surface of the island and dug.

The whole island rocked under him. It reeled and shook and one end of it rose in a hill letting out a great roar of pain.

"Earthquake!" shouted Thor Nogson.

The hill turned on them and it was a great head with fierce whiskers and long sharp teeth.

"I say, do you mind?" it said. "That hurt!"

It was a gigantic walrus. Noggin knew there was only one walrus in the world as big as that. They had met Arup, King of the Walruses.

They greeted each other as kings do and

Noggin offered his guest refreshment . . . "A ship's biscuit perhaps?"

"A ship's biscuit?" said the Walrus. "Why, yes, that would be nice. I'm feeling a bit peckish."

Noggin's men went below and brought up a chest of biscuits.

"How would you like them?" asked Noggin.

"Oh just throw them in, throw them in," replied the King of the Walruses and he opened his mouth.

Noggin and his men picked up ship's biscuits and threw them into the great mouth until the chest was empty. Then the Walrus closed his mouth and chewed.

"Mm, delicious, haven't had ship's biscuit for years!"

"Hi, what about me?" shouted Thor Nogson.

"Throw him a biscuit somebody," said Noggin.

"No! I want to come back on board! You can't leave me on this monster all day!"

"Manners, Thor Nogson, manners!" said

Noggin severely. "Wait till the King of the Walruses has finished his elevenses."

The walrus chewed another box of ship's biscuits with great pleasure and then offered to help them on their way.

"I am going towards the land of the Midnight Sun. If you just throw your gardener here a rope, I will give you a tow."

They threw Thor Nogson a rope. He tied it around the walrus's neck and quickly climbed back on board.

"Right away!" called Noggin. The walrus moved away through the calm water pulling the ship behind him.

Swiftly he swam. All that day and night he swam. Through the next day and night he pulled the little ship until they were past the black ice at the edge of the world. Then he stopped.

"I'll be off now," he said. "I go South here, but there is a good wind. Keep the Midday Sun

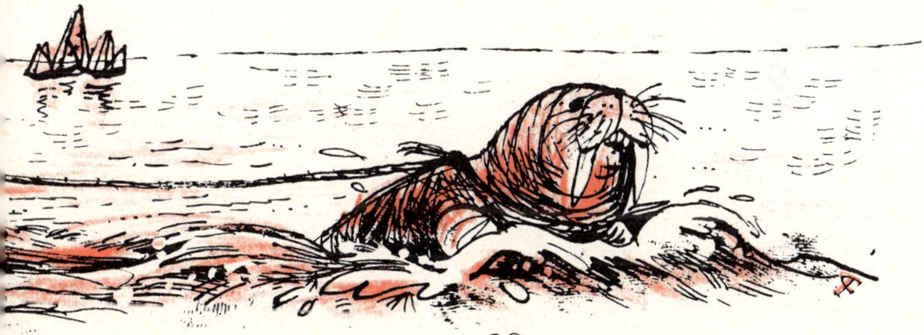

behind you. Watch out for icebergs. Good luck!"

The King of the Walruses sank beneath the waves.

The wind bore them on. That night the snow began to fall. Graculus climbed on to the prow of the ship and guided them past the icebergs while the Nogs took turns bringing him mugs of cocoa. Then, as dawn came, they saw before them the land of the Midnight Sun. It was a flat land. No mountains and forests like their own homeland, just flat ice and snow.

Nan of the Nooks was waiting for them on the shore. He was a little man in a fur hood sitting on a throne made of blocks of ice. He was surrounded by other little men in fur hoods all jumping about with excitement.

"Greetings, Noggin the Nog. Do you come in

peace?" he called.

"Hail, Nan of the Nooks. We come in peace," called Noggin the Nog as he leapt ashore.

Nan of the Nooks came down from his throne of ice and shook Noggin by the hand. "Perishing cold isn't it?" he said. "Come up to my place and have a cup of something hot."

Nan of the Nooks led Noggin to one of the round ice houses and went indoors. There was no door, only a sort of arched tunnel to crawl through. Inside, the house was bright and warm with a skin on the floor for a carpet. Nan and Noggin sat on stools and Nan's daughter brought them black tea in silver mugs.

She was Nooka, the girl whose likeness was carved on the bone knife. Noggin looked at her and she was more beautiful than he had expected.

Noggin turned to her father, he said: "Nan of the Nooks, I have come far, through hail

and wind, through snowstorm and sea mist, past the black ice at the edge of the world to ask your daughter to marry me."

"Yes, I know," said Nan of the Nooks.

"Well, er . . ." Noggin faltered, "now I'm here I feel a bit shy. Would you ask her for me?"

Nan of the Nooks laughed. "All right then."

He called his daughter. "Nooka," he said.

"Noggin has come through hail and wind through snowstorm and sea mist, past the black ice at the edge of the world to ask you to marry him. Will you marry him and be Queen of the Nogs?"

"Yes father, I will."

So Noggin and Nooka were married. There was great feasting and merriment in the land of the Midnight Sun. Fireworks lit up the sky and the Nogs and the Nooks sang their drinking songs and ate roasted caribou meat.

The next morning Graculus came to Noggin and Nooka and told them he was going to fly back to the land of Nog and tell the news that Noggin was married and on his way home. Otherwise Nogbad the Bad was sure to try and seize the throne. So Graculus flew away from the land of the Midnight Sun. Noggin, Nan and Nooka stood and waved until his strong green wings had carried him out of sight.

Far away, in the land of Nog, Nogbad the Bad stood in his black castle and looked out across the sea.

High in the air he saw a bird, a green bird, flying very slowly, like a bird that is very tired. He watched the bird flutter down and with the last of its strength land on top of the flag pole, fold its wings, tuck away its head and go to sleep.

Nogbad took hold of the flag-rope and told his guards to haul down the flag.

The guards pulled down the flag and as they did so, Nogbad was pulled up the other side of the pole.

He reached the top and grabbed the bird by the throat.

"Aaark!" cried Graculus.

"Lower away, guards," said Nogbad.

They lowered him. He held out the bird to the guards. He said: "Take this and put it in the dungeon."

The guards took Graculus and put him in a dungeon. He sat there with a bowl of water and a bowl of bird-seed and he wept. The

days passed. Then one day the door was thrown open and there stood Nogbad in purple robes carrying a golden crown.

"Look at me, bird," he said. "It is six weeks since Noggin went away. He has not returned and so, today, I go down to the council of elders in the town and they have to proclaim me King!"

Graculus watched from the barred window of the dungeon. He saw Nogbad set out in a golden carriage.

A robin perched on the window sill.

"Robin," said Graculus. "Do you want Nogbad to be king?"

The robin shook its head.

"Take this feather," said Graculus. "Put it in the hand of Queen Grunhilda and tell her I am here."

Down in the town, Nogbad the Bad drove in state past the crowds of silent people. Nobody cheered or smiled but Nogbad did not care. He thought of the royal treasure and the taxes and he smiled to himself.

In the royal castle, Queen Grunhilda stood alone by her window and looked out across the cold sea.

"Alas, my poor Noggin!" she sighed and stretched out her hand towards the horizon.

A robin landed on her hand. It was carrying a green feather.

"This is one of Graculus's feathers," said the old queen. "Where is he?"

The robin pointed with its wing towards Nogbad's castle.

The queen wasted no time. She called the guards.

"Take horses and go to the castle of Nogbad the Bad. Graculus is imprisoned there. This bird will show you the place. I am going down to the council of elders to deal with Nogbad."

At the council of elders, Nogbad was explaining what a good king he was going to be and how many extra taxes everybody would pay.

Queen Grunhilda entered the hall. "Nogbad!" she cried in ringing tones. "What is the penalty for obstructing the king's messenger?"

"The penalty is banishment, Grunhilda."

"Nogbad," she commanded, "go and pack your bags!"

The council of elders laughed, but Nogbad

twirled his moustache and scowled.

"Madam," he began. "I could have you thrown into the dungeons for insolence, but as you were once Queen of the Nogs I will be merciful. I will let you go back to your castle, but you must stay there and mind your own business, for I am the king."

"Oh no you are not." came a voice from the doorway. There was Graculus perched on the shoulder of the captain of the Queen's Guard.

"Slink away Nogbad, your time is up!" and Nogbad slunk away.

"Smoke!" cried the boy who sold winkles.

"Smoke!" cried the harbour-master.

The signal fire on the headland was burning

to show that a sail had been sighted.

They saw a ship. It was tiny and far away, but Grunhilda, looking through the harbour-master's telescope, could make out the crest of Noggin and the face of Nooka embroidered on the sail.

Soon the ship sailed up the fjord to the harbour, where, amid great rejoicing, Noggin and Nooka stepped ashore to be greeted by

their people.

Graculus told Noggin of Nogbad's wickedness and he sent soldiers to seek him out. They did not find him. Nogbad had put on his climbing boots and set off over the pass to stay with his granny in Finland.

So Noggin and Nooka came home to their kingdom.

They were crowned that day in the royal castle, Noggin and Nooka, King and Queen of the Nogs, and their reign was long and happy.